RAF, Dominion & Allied Squadrons at War:

Study, History and Statistics

Compiled by
Phil H. Listemann

Drawings by Claveworks Graphic

Preface

The purpose of this study is to provide aviation historians and enthusiasts with a range of information relative to each of the Commonwealth squadrons that saw combat during World War II. Each record will comprise a short history, complete with illustrations and artwork, and accompanied by the following appendices:

Appendix I: Squadron Commanders and Flight Commanders
Appendix II: Major awards
Appendix III: Operational diary (number of sorties per month)
Appendix IV: Victory list
Appendix V: Aircraft losses on operations
Appendix VI: Aircraft losses in accidents
Appendix VII: Aircraft Serial numbers matching with individual letters (including mission totals for multi-engine aircraft)
Appendix VIII: Nominal roll (Captains only for bomber and seaplane units)
Appendix IX: Roll of Honour

Individual files will be constantly updated, when any fresh information comes to light. Additional information will be available for download, at no charge, on each squadron's site at:

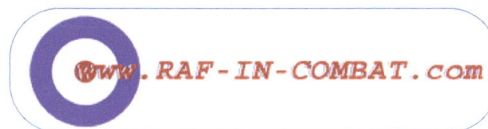

www.raf-in-combat.com

Glossary of Terms

RANKS

AC: Aircraftman	DFM: Distinguished Flying Medal
G/C: Group Captain	DSO: Distinguished Service Order
W/C: Wing Commander	Eva.: Evaded
S/L: Squadron Leader	Inj.: Injured
F/L: Flight Lieutenant	ORB: Operational Record Book
F/O: Flying Officer	OTU: Operational Training Unit
P/O: Pilot Officer	PAF: Polish Air Force
W/O: Warrant Officer	PoW: Prisoner of War
F/Sgt: Flight Sergeant	RAF: Royal Air Force
Sgt: Sergeant	RAAF: Royal Australian Air Force
Cpl: Corporal	RCAF: Royal Canadian Air Force
LAC: Leading Aircraftman	RNZAF: Royal New Zealand Air Force
	SAAF: South African Air Force
OTHER	Sqn: Squadron
AAF: Auxiliary Air Force	TOC: Taken on charge
CO: Commanding Officer	†: Killed
DFC: Distinguished Flying Cross	

No. 443 (RCAF) Squadron 1944-1946

ISBN: 978-2-918590-62-0

Contributors & Acknowledgments:
Hugh Halliday, Malcolm Laird, Chris Thomas, Roger Wallsgrove (Text consultant)

Cover: S/L Art Sager (with clipped wings Spitfire) beats up Flying Control for the benefit of an official photographer.

MAIN EQUIPMENT

SPITFIRE V	Feb.44 - Mar.44
SPITFIRE IX	Mar.44 - Mar.45
SPITFIRE XVI	Jan.45 - Jan.46
SPITFIRE XIV	Jan.46 - Mar.46

SQUADRON CODE LETTERS:

2I

SQUADRON HISTORY

No.443 (RCAF) Squadron was the last RCAF overseas squadron to be formed. It began life as No.127 Squadron, RCAF on 1 July 1942, based in Nova Scotia (Canada) and was employed to defend the East Coast of Canada with Hurricanes. At the end of 1943, it was selected as one of six home fighter units for European service. During 18 months in Canada personnel had racked up close to 800 sorties for the loss of a single aircraft and pilot, and it was this experience that made the unit a candidate for an overseas assignment.

Arriving in the United Kingdom early in 1944, complete in personnel but devoid of aircraft, it was placed under Fighter Command authority and re-designated No.443 Squadron on **8 February 1944**. It received Spitfire Mk.Vs as initial equipment to re-train the pilots, then with Spitfire Mk.IXs in April, and the Squadron was placed under 2nd TAF authority in preparation for D-Day. The CO chosen to lead this unit in combat was S/L 'Wally' McLeod, one of the most outstanding Canadian fighter pilot of that time who had made his reputation over Malta two years before. Reinforced with experienced pilots, the training continued in the first half of April until the first operation was carried out on 13 April 44, a mission escorting Bostons over Dieppe. By that time it had become part of No.144 (RCAF) Wing, with two others Canadian squadrons, Nos.441 and 442. It didn't take long before the score of the Squadron was open when S/L McLeod shot down a Do217 six days later. By D-Day, the Squadron had claimed three more victories including one by the CO. On 6 June 1944 some 48 sorties were carried out and the Squadron was intensively used over the beaches during the next few weeks. However the Squadron was badly hit on the 16 June when it lost four Spitfires and three pilots against German fighters of which two were claimed as destroyed in return. Leading the Squadron, 'Wally' McLeod soon became the top-scoring ace of the unit and added six more victories until his death at the end of September over Arnhem, three weeks after being awarded the DSO. By that time the Squadron was located in the Netherlands and had passed under No.127 (RCAF) Wing. At the end of the year, the Squadron began to receive Spitfire Mk.XVIs more suitable to ground attack missions and in 1945 alone, the Squadron carried out over 2,000 ground attack sorties to harrass German positions of all kinds. The last offensive sorties were recorded on 4 May 1945 and the very last ones four days later. But all this had a cost, with 15 aircraft lost and four pilots killed in action in 1945.

After VE-Day, the squadron became part of the Occupation force, still flying Spitfire Mk.XVIs, later replaced by Griffon-engined Spitfire Mk.XIVs, before the unit was disbanded on **15 March 1946**. During the 13 months of operations, the Squadron had flown over 5,700 sorties and had claimed 38 victories for the loss of 9 pilots KIA or MIA and 3 PoWs.

SQUADRON BASES

Digby	08.02.44 - 18.03.44	Melsbroek/B58 (Belgium)	22.10.44 - 04.11.44
Holmsley South	18.03.44 - 27.03.44	Evere/B56 (Belgium)	04.11.44 - 18.12.44
Hutton Cranswick	27.03.44 - 08.04.44	Warmwell	18.12.44 - 03.01.45
Westhampnett	08.04.44 - 22.04.44	Evere/B56 (Belgium)	03.01.45 - 03.03.45
Funtington	22.04.44 - 15.05.44	Petit Brogel/B90 (Belgium)	03.03.45 - 31.03.45
Ford	15.05.44 - 15.06.44	Eindhoven/B78 (Netherlands)	31.03.45 - 12.04.45
Ste-Croix sur Mer/B3 (France)	15.06.44 - 15.07.44	Goch/B100 (Germany)	12.04.45 - 13.04.45
Bazenville/B2 (France)	15.07.44 - 28.08.44	Diepholz/B114 (Germany)	13.04.45 - 28.04.45
Illiers-l'Evêque/B26 (France)	28.08.44 - 21.09.44	Reinsehlen/B154 (Germany)	28.04.45 - 02.07.45
Le Culot/B68 (Belgium)	21.09.44 - 30.09.44	Fassberg/B152 (Germany)	02.07.45 - 07.07.45
Grave/B82 (Netherlands)	30.09.44 - 22.10.44	Utersen/B174 (Germany)	07.07.45 - 15.03.46

ARTICLE XV

Shortly after Britain's declaration of war, supported on the same date by Australia and New Zealand, and Canada a week later, the British Government asked Commonwealth countries to supply partially trained aircrew for the expansion of the RAF. In those years prior to the war an allocation of men from the Dominions had been offered Short Service, or Permanent, Commission in the RAF, but the speed with which the Nazis had overrun Poland, made it clear that large numbers of airmen would be needed urgently. In November 1939, the Ottawa (Canada) Conference formulated the setting-up of the Empire Air Training Scheme (EATS) to train aircrew to a uniform standard in each of the Dominions previously mentioned, and subsequently South Africa, which was already operating a scheme, and Rhodesia.

Desirous of exercising some control over its own nationals, which was not the case for those who had joined up prior to the war, Canada obtained, via Article XV, an agreement that their aircrew would be gathered together in national squadrons, to serve alongside the permanent units of the RAF. For operational and administrative reasons Australia and New Zealand were reluctant to establish and maintain RAAF or RNZAF squadrons in Britain so eventually it was decided that units formed in the RAF would be identified with them.

In order to distinguish those units created under Article XV the RAF reserved a block of numbers commencing with 400 which was allocated to them. The RCAF squadrons were to start with 400, the RAAF, 450 and the RNZAF, 485. From the start aircrew were paid at the rates of pay in force in their respective countries, and depended on the RAF for aircraft and logistical support.

Their operational deployment was to be determined by the RAF, even though respective Governments of each of the Dominions retained an overview on their airmen. Some existing squadrons were re-numbered in the new series to avoid confusion with established RAF units. As an example No.1 Squadron RCAF, which was sent to support Great Britain in 1940, was subsequently re-numbered No.401 (RCAF) Squadron. The policy behind Article XV Squadrons provided a greater national identity to those countries who were able to identify themselves in their title e.g. No.443 (RCAF) Squadron.

Initially the RAF supplied the vast majority of the ground personnel for most of the Commonwealth squadrons. The aircrew posted to these squadrons represented only some, and not all, of that particular country's nationals. Indeed almost every squadron in the RAF at some time or another had members amongst their ranks from all of the Dominions- aircrew were sent where there was the greatest need for them.

In the beginning the authorities attempted to relocate serving RAF officers to those newly formed squadrons from their Dominions. However this was not always possible or practical, especially where senior positions needed to be filled. As a result British or other nationals frequently filled the vacancies in these squadrons. Regrettably friction between nationalities sometimes occurred, although this was not a major problem. The posting or replacement of certain personnel would generally defuse such situations.

By the end of the war Article XV Squadrons had proved that they were equal to the best that the RAF had produced and had no need to be envious of their British counterparts. Not only had they achieved impressive operational records but they gave the Dominions a renewed confidence and pride in their military ability.

Of the Dominions Canada became the biggest contributor, providing 44 operational squadrons between 1941 and 1944. Eight of these were sourced from Home RCAF squadrons, and, of the 44 squadrons, thirteen were of the day-fighter type.

APPENDIX I
SQUADRON AND FLIGHT COMMANDERS

Rank and Name	SN	Origin	Dates
S/L Henry W. **McLeod** *(†)*	Can./J.4912	RCAF	13.02.44 - 27.09.44
S/L Arthur H. **Sager**	Can./J.8638	RCAF	30.09.44 - 29.03.45
S/L Thomas J. **De Courcy** *(†)*	Can./J.17641	RCAF	29.03.45 - 07.06.45
S/L Hartland R. **Finley**	Can./J.14030	RCAF	08.06.45 - 17.09.45
S/L Cal D. **Bricker**	Can./J.1449	RCAF	18.09.45 - 21.03.46

A FLIGHT

F/L Ian R. **MacLennan** *(†)*	Can./J.15928	RCAF	13.02.44 - 07.06.44
F/L Frederick A.W.J. **Wilson**	Can./J.85676	RCAF	07.06.44 - 09.07.44
F/L Joseph G.L. **Robillard**	Can./J.15296	RCAF	09.07.44 - 24.09.44
F/L Easson B. **Stovel**	Can./J.7815	RCAF	24.09.44 - 12.11.44
F/L Philip G. **Blades**	Can./J.6371	RCAF	12.11.44 - 19.02.45
F/L Lloyd E. **Hunt**	Can./J.15831	RCAF	19.02.45 - 28.03.45
F/L Gervais B. **Warman**	Can./J.18540	RCAF	28.03.45 - 17.07.45
?			
F/L William T.H. **Gill**	Can./J.7766	RCAF	02.11.45 - 21.03.46

B FLIGHT

F/L William A. **Prest**	Can./J.15101	RCAF	16.02.44 - 27.07.44
F/L Gordon W. **Troke**	Can./J.15777	RCAF	27.07.44 - 16.10.44
F/L Harlan P. **Fuller**	Can./J.17752	RCAF	16.10.44 - 30.01.45
F/L Donald M. **Walz**	Can./C.12586	RCAF	30.01.45 - 24.02.45
F/L Harold C. **Charlesworth**	Can./J.15146	RCAF	24.02.45 - 28.03.45
F/L Hartland R. **Finlay**	Can./J.14030	RCAF	28.03.45 - 01.07.45
F/L Arthur van **Rensselaer-Sainsbury**	Can./J.25360	RCAF	01.07.45 - 18.10.45
F/L Frank E.W. **Hanton**	Can./J.10116	RCAF	18.10.45 - 21.03.46

APPENDIX II
MAJOR AWARDS

DSO: 1
Henry Wallace **McLeod** (Can./J.4912 - RCAF)

DFC: 5
Thomas Joseph **De Courcy** (Can./J.17641 - RCAF)
Hartland Ross **Finley** (Can./J.14030 - RCAF)
Rooney Alexander **Hodgins** (Can./J.41894 - RCAF)
Gordon Frederick **Ockenden** (Can./J.21398 - RCAF)
Arthur Hazelton **Sager** (Can./J.8638 - RCAF)

DFM: -

APPENDIX III
OPERATIONAL DIARY
NUMBER OF SORTIES PER MONTH

Date	Month	Total	Date	Month	Total
Apr.44	189	189			
May.44	256	445	Jan.45	163	3,793
Jun.44	552	997	Feb.45	327	4,120
Jul.44	743	1,740	Mar.45	597	4,717
Aug.44	726	2,466	Apr.45	831	5,548
Sep.44	261	2,727	May.45	184	5,732
Oct.44	556	3,283			
Nov.44	203	3,486	**Grand Total**		**5,732**
Dec.44	144	3,630			

Extracted from AIR27/1883

APPENDIX IV
VICTORY LIST
CONFIRMED (C) AND PROBABLE (P) CLAIMS

Date	Pilot	SN	Origin	Type	Serial	Code	Nb	Cat.
				SPITFIRE IX				
19.04.44	S/L Henry W. McLeod	Can./J.4912	RCAF	Do217	MK321	2I-H	1.0	C
25.04.44	F/L Donald M. Walz	Can./C.12586	RCAF	Fw190	MK605	2I-W	1.0	C
	F/L Hugh Russell	Can./J.5818	RCAF	Fw190	MJ741	2I-X	1.0	C
05.05.44	S/L Henry W. McLeod	Can./J.4912	RCAF	Fw190	MK636	2I-E	1.0	C
07.06.44	F/L Hugh Russell	Can./J.5818	RCAF	Bf109	n/k	2I-Z	0.5	C
	F/O Gordon F. Ockenden	Can./J.21398	RCAF		n/k	2I-U	0.5	C
14.06.44	S/L Henry W. McLeod	Can./J.4912	RCAF	Do217	MK636	2I-E	1.0	C
	F/O Rooney A. Hodgins	Can./J.41894	RCAF	Do217	NH300	2I-V	1.0	P
16.06.44	F/L Donald M. Walz	Can./C.12586	RCAF	Bf109	MK605	2I-W	1.0	C
	S/L Henry W. McLeod	Can./J.4912	RCAF	Bf109	MK636	2I-E	1.0	C
23.06.44	S/L Henry W. McLeod	Can./J.4912	RCAF	Fw190	MK636	2I-E	2.0	C
28.06.44	F/O Gordon R. Stephen	Can./J.18775	RCAF	Fw190	ML153	2I-W	1.0	C
	F/O Wiiliam A.C. Gilbert	Can./J.29310	RCAF	Fw190	MK315	2I-C	1.0	C
20.07.44	S/L Henry W. McLeod	Can./J.4912	RCAF	Fw190	MK636	2I-E	1.0	C
	F/L Joseph G.L. Robillard	Can./J.15296	RCAF	Fw190	MK315	2I-C	1.0	C
26.07.44	F/O Gordon R. Stephen	Can./J.18775	RCAF	Fw190	ML153	2I-W	1.0	C
30.07.44	S/L Henry W. McLeod	Can./J.4912	RCAF	Bf109	MK636	2I-E	1.0	C
	F/O William J. Bentley	Can./J.18928	RCAF	Bf109	NH244	2I-R	1.0	C
08.08.44	F/L Gordon W.A. Troke	Can./J.15777	RCAF	Bf109	ML184	2I-P	0.25	C
	F/O Walter J. Sherman	Can./J.18283	RCAF		MJ171	2I-V	0.25	C
	F/O Arthur J. Horrell	Can./J.21413	RCAF		NH208	2I-Z	0.25	C
	F/O Daniel W. Wegg	Can./J.39826	RCAF		NH244	2I-R	0.25	C
23.08.44	F/O Gordon F. Ockenden	Can./J.21398	RCAF	Bf109	MJ799	2I-X	2.0	C
	F/O Arthur J. Horrell	Can./J.21413	RCAF	Fw190	MJ779		1.0	C
	F/L Joseph G.L. Robillard	Can./J.15296	RCAF	Bf109	MK315	2I-C	1.0	C

Date	Pilot		S/N	Origin	Type	Serial	Code	Mark		Fate
27.09.44	F/L Donald M. **WALZ**		CAN./C.12586	RCAF	Bf109	**MJ660**		1.0	C
	F/O Wiiliam A.C. **GILBERT**		CAN./J.29310	RCAF	Bf109	**MJ477**	2I-J	1.0	C
	F/L Easson B. **STOVEL**		CAN./J.7815	RCAF	Bf109	**MK315**	2I-C	1.0	C
					Bf109	**MK315**	2I-C	1.0	P
	F/L Harlan P. **FULLER**		CAN./J.17752	RCAF	Bf109	**NH157**	2I-Z	1.0	C
	F/O Rooney A. **HODGINS**		CAN./J.41894	RCAF	Bf109	**ML153**	2I-W	1.0	P
29.09.44	F/O Arthur J. **HORRELL**		CAN./J.21413	RCAF	Fw190	**NH208**	2I-V	1.0	C
	F/O Gordon F. **OCKENDEN**		CAN./J.21398	RCAF	Bf109	**MJ171**		2.0	C
	F/O Rooney A. **HODGINS**		CAN./J.41894	RCAF	Bf109	**ML417**	2I-T	2.0	C
	F/L Gordon W.A. **TROKE**		CAN./J.15777	RCAF	Bf109	**NH157**	2I-N	2.0	C

SPITFIRE XVI

Date	Pilot		S/N	Origin	Type	Serial	Code		Fate	
02.05.45	P/O Montagne J.S. **CLOW**		CAN./J.42132	RCAF	Ju88	**TD282**		0.5	C
	F/L Hartland R. **FINLEY**		CAN./J.14030	RCAF		**TD293**		0.5	C
03.05.45	F/O William A.S. **MARSHALL**		CAN./J.44843	RCAF	Ju88	**TB522**		0.33	C
	F/L Raymond G. **SIM**		CAN./J.6947	RCAF		**SM345**		0.33	C
	S/L Thomas J. DE **COURCY**		CAN./J.17641	RCAF		**TD239**	2I-C	0.33	C

Total: 38.0

Aircraft damaged: 12.0

APPENDIX V
AIRCRAFT LOST ON OPERATIONS

Date	Pilot	S/N	Origin	Serial	Code	Mark	Fate

SPITFIRE

25.04.44	F/O Edmund H. **FAIRFIELD**	CAN/J.20013	RCAF	**MK212**		LF.IX	-

Took off at 07.25 with eight others for a sweep into the Paris area. Ran out of fuel after combat with enemy aircraft and crash-landed near Warmwell, Dorset. Pilot was uninjured. Canadian from Ontario, Edmund Fairfield was with No.127 Sqn, RCAF between July and September 1942 before being posted to No.129 Sqn, RCAF. After having served with No.128 Sqn, RCAF he returned to No.127 Sqn, RCAF in April 1943 and was posted overseas with the Squadron in January 1944. He left the Squadron in March 1945 as tour-expired and was repatriated in August 1945. (See also operational losses 13.01.45)

Note on the aircraft: TOC No.9 MU 28.01.44, issued No.443 Sqn 11.03.44.

	P/O Philip G. **BOCKMAN**	CAN./J.40106	(US)/RCAF	**MK321**	2I-H	LF.IX	-

See above. Injured, he was admitted to the military hospital at Bovington. 'Phil' Bockman was an American citizen who enlisted in the RCAF in September 1941 and was an original member of the Squadron. He served with No.126 Sqn, RCAF between July and October 1942 then with No.127 Sqn, RCAF from October 1942 onwards. Recovering, he rejoined the Squadron in September 1944 and was eventually repatriated in September 1945.

Note on the aircraft: TOC No.9 MU 12.02.44, issued No.443 Sqn 11.03.44.

07.06.44	F/L Ian R. **MACLENNAN**	CAN./J.15928	RCAF	**MH850**	2I-H	LF.IX	**PoW**

Took off for with 12 others at 11.25, the CO leading, for a patrol over the British beach-head. Engine failure in flight due to glycol leak and crash-landed in an enemy controlled area. F/O Piché, his No.2, reported having circled the field at 100 feet but was forced to leave after a few minutes as the enemy's guns were making it difficult for him. The position was two miles west of Cabourg, beside the shore. The aircraft was considerably damaged by striking prepared obstacles in the field but F/L MacLennan was seen to climb from the cockpit and run west towards farm buildings and was taken prisoner, being held in custody at Stalag

Luft III. Canadian from Saskatchewan he was serving overseas from July 1941, first with No.610 Sqn (February – April 1942), then with No.401 (RCAF) Sqn until May when he volunteered to serve at Malta where he flew with No.1435 Sqn. He returned to the UK at the end of the year and was posted to No.443 in February 1944 as Flight Commander. His tally rose to seven confirmed victories and eight damaged and he was awarded the DFM [No.1435 Sqn]. He was eventually repatriated in July 1945, retiring the following October.

Note on the aircraft: TOC No.39 MU 01.10.43. Served with No.411 (RCAF) Sqn before to be issued No.443 Sqn at an unrecorded date but the ORB gives a first trace early in May 1944. It was probably one the aircraft sent to replace the losses which occurred at the end of April.

07.06.44   F/O Robert B. **HENDERSON**   CAN./J.16753   RCAF   **MJ455**   2I-R   LF.IX   -

Took off at 19.45 with 11 other to patrol over the British beach area, S/L J.D. Hall leading. Engine failure in flight when he switched from the overload tank to the main tank. The aircraft was seen to break up badly but the pilot was able to climb out and move away from the aircraft. He returned to the Squadron two days later. Canadian from Ontario, he completed a first tour in the UK between July 1941 and June 1943 before being repatriated. He served as a flying instructor with No.1 OTU at Bagotville before being posted overseas a second time in February 1944, joining No.443 Sqn, and left the Squadron on completion of his tour in February 1945. Repatriated the following month, he left the RCAF in May the same year.

Note on the aircraft: TOC No.33 MU 16.11.43, issued No.443 Sqn 13.03.44.

16.06.44   S/L James D. **HALL**   CAN./C.1624   RCAF   **MK397**   2I-T   LF.IX   †

Took off at 20.35 with 17 others, Hall leading a formation of six, while McLeod and J.E.J. Johnston led the 12 others (6 each). Hall's formation was bounced by Fw190s and Hall was shot down. All four aircraft were last seen by the two survivors climbing into clouds at 3,000 feet north of Caen over the Canal as a very thick barrage of flak was being thrown up. Hall, a regular RCAF officer, had been posted in as supernumerary Squadron Leader at the end of May 1944 for a second tour, pending another posting as CO. He had served overseas from April 1942, first with No.421 Sqn in August and September 1942 then to No.416 Sqn (September – December 1942) and No.402 Sqn (December 1942 – April 1943) before returning to No.421 Sqn as CO in April 1943 until June. Before his second tour he served with RCAF Overseas Headquarters. While CO of No.421 Sqn, Hall had claimed one confirmed victory.

Note on the aircraft: TOC No.9 MU 07.02.44, issued No.443 Sqn 13.03.44.

F/L Donald M. **WALZ**   CAN./C.12586   RCAF   **MK605**   2I-W   LF.IX   **Eva.**

As above. Walz evaded capture and rejoined the unit later on. Donald Walz was a Canadian from Saskatchewan who had previously served with No.126 Sqn, RCAF in July 1942, then with No.127 Sqn, RCAF from July 1942 onwards and was posted over seas with the Squadron early 1944 where it became No.443 (RCAF) Sqn. He seems to have been posted upon his arrival in the UK. (See operational losses 24.02.45)

Note on the aircraft: TOC No.9 MU 01.02.44, issued No.443 Sqn 11.03.44.

F/L Hugh **RUSSEL**   CAN./J.5818   RCAF   **NH300**   2I-V   LF.IX   †

See above. Canadian pilot from Montreal (Quebec), serving overseas since July 1941 and served with No.402 (RCAF) Sqn before joining No.416 (RCAF) as a Flight Commander in July 1942 with which he claimed a Fw190 on 19 August 1942. Repatriated in January 1943 to serve in various second line unit postings, he returned to the UK in October 1944 to join the Squadron in March 1944. It seems that he had been posted in as a supernumerary Flight Lieutenant.

Note on the aircraft: TOC No.8 MU 20.05.44, issued No.443 Sqn at an unrecorded date.

F/O Luis **PEREZ-GOMEZ**   CAN./J.29172   (MEX)/RCAF   **MK607**   2I-S   LF.IX   †

See above. Luis Perez-Gomez was a Mexican citizen who enlisted in Ottawa in June 1942 while he was studying at the Ontario Technical School. Upon completing his training he joined No.127 Sqn, RCAF in October 1943 and followed the unit to the UK. Luis Perez-Gomez was one of the few Mexicans to enlist in the RCAF and the only one to have died on operations whilst flying for the RCAF.

Note on the aircraft: TOC No.9 MU 01.02.44, issued No.443 Sqn 11.03.44.

25.07.44   F/O Thomas G. **MUNRO**   CAN./J.24592   RCAF   **MJ514**   LF.IX   **PoW**

Took off at 18.00 with 11 others for an armed reconnaissance to the Mezidon-Thury-Harcourt-Flers-Falaise area, F/L W.A. Prest leading. His engine gave trouble at 8,000 feet and the pilot tried to glide back to base but was unable to make it and abandoned the aircraft at 1,500 feet 4 m east of Villers-Bocage. Except that he was taken prisoner, his subsequent fate is obscure. It is believed that he was held in a military hospital, with no evidence of transfer to a Stalag. He was repatriated in February 1945, probably for humanitarian reasons, and he is reported to have died on 18.12.45. Canadian from the province

of Quebec, he was an original member of No.127 Sqn, RCAF serving with it from June 1943.
Note on the aircraft: TOC No.33 MU 25.11.43, issued to No.84 GSU 24.05.44 and issued to No.443 Sqn soon afterwards but no date recorded.

12.08.44   F/O William J. **Bentley**   Can./J.18928   RCAF   **ML303**   LF.IX   †
Took off at 11.14 with ten others for an armed recce over the Lisieux area. The engine failed in flight due a glycol leak and the pilot tried to bale out NW of Bernay. Unfortunately his parachute caught the top of the tail and he went in with his aircraft. Bentley was a Canadian from Ontario who was serving overseas from July 1941 and served with No.152 Sqn (November 1941 - March 1942), No.65 Sqn (March 1942 - October 1942) and No.249 Sqn in Mediterannean (December 1942 - April 1943) for his first tour. Bentley had joined the Squadron in May 1944 but without clear orders and was later on posted for two days to No.441 Sqn in June before returning to No.443 Sqn due to the severe losses sustained by the Squadron on 16th June.
Note on the aircraft: TOC No.33 MU 08.05.44, issued to No.83 GSU 16.05.44 and issued to No.443 Sqn soon afterwards but no date recorded.

26.09.44   F/O Llewellyn D. **Sherwood**   Can./J.15715   RCAF   **MJ779**   LF.IX   **Eva.**
Twelve aircraft took off at 17.30 for a low cover patrol over the Arnheim area, led by the CO. Believed to have been hit by flak, he attempted to make a force landing 6 miles NW of Nijmegen. However he undershot the field and the aircraft burned out in the process. He managed to escape and was reported safe in the Allied lines one month later, but was repatriated at the end of November. 'Doughy' Sherwood was a Canadian from Nova Scotia who served overseas from August 1941, having completed a first tour with No.610 Sqn (October 1941 – February 1942) and No.127 Sqn (February 1942 – July 1943) in the Middle East. He had joined the Squadron for a second tour in August 1944.
Note on the aircraft: TOC No.33 MU 19.12.43, issued No.443 Sqn 06.08.44.

27.09.44   S/L Harry W. **McLeod**   Can./J.4912   RCAF   **NH245**   LF.IX   †
The Squadron took off at 12.20 for a high cover patrol over the Nimgen-Venlo area, W/C Johnson flying with the Squadron. Nine enemy aircraft were sighted at 1000' and 20 miles east of Nimjengen. The Squadron bounced from 9000' feet and in the ensuing combat, McLeod was posted missing. A Canadian from Saskatchewan, he served overseas from July 1941, first with No.132 Sqn, then with No.485 (NZ) Sqn and No.602 Sqn and eventually No.411 (RCAF) Sqn from December 1941 onwards. In May 1942 he sailed to Malta and joined No.603 Sqn and later No.1435 Sqn, achieving considerable successes and becoming one of the top-scorers by the time he left the island in October 1942. He was repatriated to Canada where he served as flying instructor at No.1 OTU (Bagotville) before sailing to the UK in January 1944. He was given command of the newly-formed No.443 Sqn soon after his arrival. With 21 confirmed victories and three more probablse, 'Wally' McLeod had become the Canadian top-scorer in WW2. He was also awarded a DFC & BAR [both No.1435 Flight] and the only DSO of the Squadron, gazetted on 05.09.44.
Note on the aircraft: TOC No.9 MU 09.05.44, issued to No.443 Sqn 17.08.44.

29.09.44   F/L John R. **Irwin**   Can./J.11968   RCAF   **NH347**   LF.IX   -
Twelve aircraft took off at 08.45 for a low patrol over Nijmegen led by F/L Trobe. Met about 50 Bf 109s flying lower at 3,000 feet 5 miles NW of the town and engaged the enemy aircraft. In the ensuing combat nine Spitfires were obliged to land at various places in the Allied lines mainly due to shortage of petrol, but four had being badly shot up including Irwin's aircraft which crashed near Grave. All the other aircraft were later repaired. Irwin was a Canadian from Ontario who had served in Canada with No.111 (Fighter) Sqn, RCAF in June 1942 and later with No.14 (Fighter) Sqn, RCAF from June 1942 onwards. Posted overseas in January 1944 and joined the Squadron the following month. He left in February 1945 at the end of his tour and was repatriated in August 1945.
Note on the aircraft: TOC No.8 MU 23.05.44, issued No.443 Sqn 22.06.44.

30.11.44   F/O Albert M.F. **Thomas**   Can./J.42790   RCAF   **MK611**   LF.IX   -
Six Spitfires took off at 13.25 to patrol over Woerth, led by F/L Blades. The pilot was forced to return early due to engine trouble (glycol leak) which seized and caught fire. F/O Thomas had no choice but to bale out approximately 6 miles NE of Bourg Leopold (Belgium). A Canadian from Manitoba, he had joined the Squadron in July 1944 for a second tour of operations. He had served overseas between January 1942 and October 1943 before being sent back to Canada for a time. He left the Squadron in March 1945 and was repatriated the same month.
Note on the aircraft: TOC No.9 MU 01.02.44. Served with No.603 Sqn before being issued to No.443 Sqn on 18.07.44.

03.12.44   F/O Daniel J. **Wegg**   Can./J.39826   RCAF   **MK695**   LF.IX   -

Six Spitfires led F/L Fulley took off at 07.44 for a patrol in the Weert area (Netherlands). Wegg was forced to crash-land due to engine trouble, 6 miles west of Weert. A Canadian from Ontario, Wegg had served with No.128 Sqn, RCAF between October 1942 and January 1944 before being sent overseas. He had joined the Squadron in August 1944 for his first tour and was repatriated in September 1945.

Note on the aircraft: TOC No.8 MU 27.03.44, issued No.443 Sqn 08.08.44. Had previously served with Nos.132 and 403 (RCAF) Sqns.

01.01.45   -   -   -   **MK730**   LF.IX   -

Destroyed in an air raid during Operation Bodenplate.

Note on the aircraft: TOC No.39 MU 02.03.44, issued No.443 Sqn 14.12.44. Previously served with No.403 (RCAF) Sqn.

              -   -   -   **ML153**   2I-W   LF.IX   -

Destroyed in an air raid during Operation Bodenplate.

Note on the aircraft: TOC No.6 MU 28.03.44, issued No.443 Sqn 22.06.44.

05.01.45   F/O Thomas C. **Gamey**   Can./J.28753   RCAF   **NH157**   2I-N   LF.IX   †

Six aircraft took off at 15.35 for a fighter sweep and armed recce over the Munster area with four Spitfires of No.421 Sqn, F/L Walz leading. Two factories were attacked and intense accurate light and heavy flak was encountered. Gamay was hit and was seen to crash in flames. All the others returned to base at 17.00; Thomas Gamey was a Canadian from Ontario who had served in Canada with No.125 Sqn, RCAF from August 1943, with which he was posted overseas where it became No.441 (RCAF) Sqn. He was with the Squadron since November 1944.

Note on the aircraft: TOC No.6 MU 27.04.44, issued No.443 Sqn 22.06.44.

13.01.45   F/L Edmund H. **Fairfield**   Can./J.20013   RCAF   **MJ444**   LF.IX   -

Led by S/L Sager, 13 aircraft took off at 11.52 for an armed recce over the St-Vith-Rouffalise area. METs were attacked claiming five destroyed but light flak hit Faifield's aircraft in the engine and the pilot had to bale out. He landed in the Allied lines and returned the same day with a slightly injured ankle from getting out of the cockpit. He was however able to return to operations within a couple of day. (see operational losses 25.04.44 for other details on the pilot)

Note on the aircraft: TOC No.9 MU 05.11.43. Served with Nos.403 (RCAF) at 411 (RCAF) Sqns before to be issued to No.443 Sqn on 14.12.44.

24.02.45   F/L Donald M. **Walz**   Can./C.12586   RCAF   **SM478**   2I-S   LF.XVI   **PoW**

Twelve aircraft took off at 13.15 led by Walz for an armed recce over the Muster-Ham area. The formation attacked METs of which three were destroyed, three more damaged. However the flak was accurate and Walz's aircraft was hit in radiator and a glycol leak resulted so he had to bale out over enemy territory. He was taken prisoner and was released the following May. He was repatriated in June 1945. (see also operational losses 16.06.44.)

Note on the aircraft: TOC No.39 MU 30.11.44, issued No.443 Sqn 01.02.45.

24.03.45   F/O Harold C. **Charlesworth**   Can./J.15146   RCAF   **TB481**   LF.XVI   -

At 16.25 twelve aircraft were dispatched on patrol to the Doysten-Winterswijk area. Nothing was reported and the mission was uneventful. On the way back, the engine of the Spitfire cut due to shortage of petrol and the aircraft made a force landing in Belgium in circuit of B.90 while the formation returned to base at 18.10. 'Chuck' Charlesworth was a Canadian from British Colombia and served overseas from spring 1941. He became a founder member of No.412 (RCAF) Sqn in June 1941 leaving in May 1942. He was sent to the Middle East where he flew with No.73 Sqn between September 1942 and August 1943. He was with the squadron from July 1944 and was repatriated in August 1945.

Note on the aircraft: TOC No.39 MU 10.02.45, issued No.443 Sqn at a non recorded date. It seems however that the aircraft had been issued to the Squadron a couple of days before it was lost.

31.03.45   F/O Gordon A. **McDonald**   Can./J.42948   RCAF   **SM314**   LF.XVI   -

Twelve a/c led by the CO took off at 09.50 for a patrol which was uneventful. However McDonald's aircraft seems to have suffered an engine failure and he was obliged to bale out 8m NE of Deventer. He landed safely and was rescued by civilians.

McDonald served with the RCAF then with the CAF after the war. He had joined the Squadron in February and it was the second time in the month the pilot was involved in an aircraft mishap (see accidental losses 13.03.45)
Note on the aircraft: TOC No.33 MU 04.11.44. Served with No.421 (RCAF) Sqn before to issued to No.443 Sqn on 08.02.45.

06.04.45   F/O Stanley E. **Messum**   Can./J.19447   RCAF   **SM670**   LF.XVI   †
Took off at 13.25 with three others for a weather recce over the Rheine area. The formation was caught by flak at approximately 16.10 which hit Messum's aircraft while he was at 2,000 feet. He called on the R/T that he was baling out but no chute was observed and his Spitfire was seen crashing close to woods. The rest of the formation returned to base safely at 17.05. A Canadian from Alberta, Stanley Messum served overseas from the end of 1941 and received his commission in October 1943. He had served with No.416 (RCAF) Sqn between November 1941 and March 1942, No.403 (RCAF) Sqn in March-April 1942 before he volunteered to serve in Malta where he fought with No.601 Sqn. He had joined the Squadron in March 45.
Note on the aircraft: TOC No.39 MU 04.12.44, issued No.443 Sqn 01.02.45.

21.04.45   F/L Robert D. **Marsh**   Can./J.16643   RCAF   **SM383**   2I-P   LF.XVI   **Eva.**
At 12.55 eight aircraft led by F/L T.R. Watt were despatched for an armed recce over the Parchim-Schwerin area. Around 13.30 while attacking a train, March's aircraft was hit by flak and he was seen to crash-land but he was able to evade capture. 'Swampy' March returned later to the Squadron but didn't fly on operations any more, being repatriated in September 1945. Marsh, a Canadian from Ontario, had joined the squadron in December 1944 for a second tour. He had completed a first tour in the Middle East serving with Nos.73, 33 and 94 Sqns between 1942 and 1944.
Note on the aircraft: TOC No.6 MU 09.11.44, issued No.443 Sqn 15.02.45. Had previously served with No.416 (RCAF) Sqn.

21.04.45   F/O Harry R. **Hanscom**   Can./J.88672   RCAF   **SM664**   2I-H   LF.XVI   †
Six aircraft took off at 18.05 for an armed recce over Parchim-Schwerin, F/L Watt leading. Caught by enemy fighters at 9,000 feet he was posted missing believed shot down and did not return. He was last seen orbiting at 12,000' feet over the area after combat. The rest of the formation landed back at 20.00. Hanscom had joined the Squadron in March 1945 for a second tour and as with Marsch had served in the Middle East with Nos.33 and 94 Sqns. He was a Canadian from Manitoba.
Note on the aircraft: TOC No.39 MU 07.12.44, issued No.443 Sqn 01.02.45.

22.04.45   P/O Percival C. **Gomm**   Can./J.28753   (us)/RCAF   **TD154**   LF.XVI   -
Three a/c led by F/L Charlesworth took off at 14.15 for a patrol. While patrolling at 3,000 feet, the formation was fired upon by flak, not knowing if it was friend or foe. Gomm's aircraft received a direct hit just behind the cockpit but was able to return to base at 15.40. The Spitfire was sent for repairs but after investigation and, probably because of the end of the war, it was recategorized Cat.E on 13.06.45. Percival Gomm was an American citizen who enlisted in Toronto in December 1941. He was posted overseas in March 1943 and joined No.443 Sqn in October 1944. He served with the RCAF until October 1945 when he was discharged.
Note on the aircraft: TOC No.29 MU 10.03.45, issued No.443 Sqn not recorded.

25.04.45   F/O Arthur J. **Dilworth**   Can./J.24427   RCAF   **TA739**   LF.XVI   †
Led by the CO, S/L De Courcy, eight Spitfires took off at 17.30 for an armed recce around the Stade-Bremen area. The Neustatd aerodrome was attacked where three Fw190s were claimed destroyed, two more damaged. However the flak was accurate and hit Dilworth's machine which crashed in flames. Arthur Dilworth was a Canadian from the province of Quebec and served as flying instructor in Canada in 1943 before being posted overseas in April 1944. He joined the Squadron early in the month.
Note on the aircraft: TOC No.9 MU 01.12.44, issued No.443 Sqn at an unrecorded date. Had previously served with Nos.416 (RCAF) and 403 (RCAF) Sqns.

26.04.45   F/L Terence R. **Watt**   Can./J.10399   RCAF   **SM364**   LF.XVI   **Inj.**
Eight aircraft took off at 09.55 led by Watt for an armed recce. Found and attacked METs of which nine were destroyed or damaged. He reported a glycol leak probably due to flak and would have to put down, and crash-landed NE of Bad Segeberg during which he overshot and broke up his aircraft. However he was not seen getting out but was later reported as being seriously wounded at No.52 MFH. A Canadian from Ontario, he first served as a flying instructor before being posted to operational units, No.132 Sqn, RCAF in April 1943, then No.163 Sqn, RCAF in November 1943 and eventually

No.133 Sqn, RCAF in March 1944. Posted overseas in May 1944. He had joined the Squadron in September 1944. He never returned to the Squadron and was eventually repatriated in July 1945.

Note on the aircraft: TOC No.8 MU 04.11.44, issued No.443 Sqn not recorded. Served previously with No.421 (RCAF) Sqn.

F/L William G. **CONWAY**	CAN./J.43780	(US)/RCAF	**TB923**	LF.XVI	-

See above. Conway was leading the other patrol. He called that he had hit a pole when pulling up from ground attack. His aircraft began to vibrate badly and his compass was u/s. Last heard calling for homing directions. Later reported safe. An American citizen, William Conway enlisted in the RCAF in October 1941. He served in various instructor postings in Canada before being sent overseas in April 1944. He was repatriated in July 1945.

Note on the aircraft: TOC No.33 MU 03.03.45, issued No.443 05.04.45.

P/O Horace F. **PACKARD**	CAN./J.17401	RCAF	**TB883**	LF.XVI	-

Took off at 20.15 with F/L H.R. Finlay leading for a patrol over base. On return Packard misjudged the landing path in the dusk and went off the runway onto soft ground. Pilot escaped with minor injuries. A Canadian from the Province of Quebec he first served with No.119 (BR) Sqn, RCAF on non-flying duties before starting a pilot's course in July 1941. He served overseas from March 1942, first with No.416 (RCAF) Sqn between September 1942 and May 1943 and No.421 Sqn between May 1943 and February 1944 with which he claimed one confirmed victory. He returned to Canada to serve as flying instructor and then to No.126 Sqn, RCAF between October 1944 and February 1945. He was sent again overseas and joined the Squadron in April 1945. He was repatriated in September 1945.

Note on the aircraft: TOC No.33 MU 24.02.45, issued No.443 Sqn 29.03.45.

02.05.45	F/L Hartland R. **FINLEY**	CAN./J.14030	RCAF	**TD293**	LF.XVI	-

*Led by the CO, six Spitfires took off at 15.20 for a fighter sweep over the Kiel area. They found and attacked enemy aircraft on the ground on the east shore of the lake. They claimed one Fieseler Storch and one seaplane destroyed, two more as damaged. Later one Ju88 was sighted flying north at 2,500 feet and they chased it and shot it down. However, Finley was hit by the rear gunner of the Ju88 and had to bale out at 200 feet. He returned three days later. Hartland Finlay was from Montreal (Quebec) and first served as a flying instructor in Canada before being posted overseas in 1943. He briefly served with No.1 Sqn and No.416 (RCAF) Sqn before joining No.403 (RCAF) Sqn in September that year with which he claimed two confirmed victories. He completed his first tour in May 1944. He started a second tour in February 1945 flying with No.403 (RCAF) Sqn again but was posted to No.443 Sqn on 24 April 1945. He left the Squadron in July - with a **DFC** gazetted on 24 July - for a posting to RCAF Overseas HQ and returned to Canada in October where he was released from the RCAF with four confirmed victories, one being shared.*

Note on the aircraft: TOC No.39 MU 09.04.45, issued No.443 Sqn not recorded.

OTHER TYPE
(AUSTER)

11.10.44	P/O Louis P.E. **PICHÉ**	CAN./C.25294	RCAF	**NJ669**	V	†
	F/O Arthur J. **HORRELL**	CAN./J.21413	RCAF			†

F/O Piché took off with F/O Horrell in an Auster belonging to the Wing for Antwerp where F/O Horrell was to pick up a Spitfire and F/O Piché was to continue on to Brussels to make arrangements for billets for service personnel while on leave. The Auster was actually caught by flak near Deurne while wandering over German lines.

Even with parents living in the USA, Emile Piché was a Canadian citizen from Quebec province. Regular RCAF officer, he first served as a flying instructor in Canada before being posted to No.127 Sqn, RCAF in July 1943 before sailing to the UK with the Squadron which was renamed No.443 Sqn in February 1944. Arthur Horrell was a Canadian from Ontario who alsoserved as a flying instructor in Canada before joining No.127 Sqn, RCAF in May 1943 with which he sailed to the UK in January 1944. He served briefley with No.441 (RCAF) Sqn during summer 1944.

Note on the aircraft: TOC direct by No.416 (RCAF) Sqn 19.06.44. Later served with No.127 Wing.

Total: 33
(including one non-combat aircraft)

SPITFIRE

08.03.45 F/O Joseph C. **TURCOTT** CAN./J.18713 RCAF **TB621** LF.XVI -
Clarence Turcott had been sent to collect a Spitfire for the Squadron. The flight was uneventful and he had landed at 16.45 at Petit Brogel when he was hit by another Spitfire Mk.XVI (TB634) of No.403 (RCAF) Sqn hit coming in too close behind him. TB621 was badly damaged and was declared non repairable on 28.03.45 (but TB634 was repaired). Turcott had joined the Squadron in February 1945 and had been serving overseas since August 1942, first with No.421 (RCAF) Sqn until March 1943 when he was injured after a force-landing following an engine failure on take-off on the 6th. It seems that he didn't return to the 421. 'Turk' Turcott was posted to No.421 Sqn again in July 1945 and was repatriated in August 1945. He was a Canadian from Ontario.
Note on the aircraft: TOC No.29 MU 03.02.45, issued No.443 Sqn a couple of days before (no date available).

13.03.45 F/O Gordon A. **McDONALD** CAN./J.42948 RCAF **SM469** LF.XVI -
McDonald took off at 16.50 for an aircraft test flight, when on return half an hour later, he made an heavy landing causing a tyre to burst. The aircraft swung and hit sand at the side of the runway causing the aircraft to tip on its nose. (see operational losses 31.03.45 for more details on the pilot)
Note on the aircraft: TOC No.6 MU 23.11.44, issued No.443 Sqn 13.01.45.

19.04.45 - - - **SM189** LF.XVI -
Engine caught fire during ground running, Diepholz.
Note on the aircraft: TOC No.8 MU 30.10.44, issued No.443 Sqn 01.02.45.

15.09.45 - - - **TB501** LF.XVI -
Destroyed on the ground when a containers dropped by a Stirling during a supply dropping sortie struck the Spitfire by mistake.
Note on the aircraft: TOC No.29 MU 03.02.45. First issued to No.66 Sqn before to be issued No.443 Sqn 21.07.45.

18.01.46 F/L Nicholas H. **RASSENTI** CAN./J.22462 RCAF **TB915** LF.XVI -
During a training flight, the formation of three Spitfires led by F/L Burnett flying at 4000 feet was 'attacked' by a USAAF Thunderbolt (P-47D-30-RA 44-33258) but the pilot - Capt Stewart R. Brown - misjudged his approach and hit Ressenti's aircraft. Both pilots baled out safely. Nicholas Rassenti was a Canadian from Ontario who had served in Canada with No.123 (Army Cooperation) Sqn, RCAF between January and December 1943 before being posted overseas where he joined No.439 (RCAF) Sqn on Typhoons with which he completed a tour. He had joined the Squadron in December 1945 and was repatriated again in June 1946. Rassenti served with the post-war RCAF.
Note on the aircraft: TOC No.19 MU 27.02.45. First issued to Nos.66, 421 (RCAF) & 416 (RCAF) Sqns Sqn before to be issued No.443 Sqn 15.11.45.

Total: 5

APPENDIX VII
Aircraft serial numbers matching with individual letters

2I-A
MA329 (*Spitfire IX*)

2I-B
TB269 (*Spitfire XVI*)
NH922 (*Spitfire XIV*)

2I-C
MK315 (*Spitfire IX*)
TB923, TD239 (*Spitfire XVI*)

2I-D
MJ340 (*Spitfire IX*)
TB476 (*Spitfire XVI*)

2I-E
MK636 (*Spitfire IX*)
SM467 (*Spitfire XVI*)

2I-F
SM485 (*Spitfire XVI*)

2I-G
TA741 (*Spitfire XVI*)

2I-H
MH850, MK321 (*Spitfire IX*)
SM664 (*Spitfire XVI*)

2I-I

2I-J
MJ366, MJ477 (*Spitfire IX*)
SM204 (*Spitfire XVI*)

2I-K

2I-L

2I-M
MJ334 (*Spitfire IX*)
TZ198 (*Spitfire XIV*)

2I-N
MH370, NH157 (*Spitfire IX*)
SM512 (*Spitfire XVI*)

2I-O
NH998, NH178 (*Spitfire IX*)

2I-P
ML184 (*Spitfire IX*)
SM383, TD191 (*Spitfire XVI*)

2I-Q

2I-R
MJ455, NH244, NH411
(*Spitfire IX*)
SM646 (*Spitfire XVI*)

2I-S
MK607, ML194 (*Spitfire IX*)
SM478 (*Spitfire XVI*)

2I-T
MK397, ML417 (*Spitfire IX*)
SM329 (*Spitfire XVI*)

2I-U

2I-V
MJ171, MJ387, MK356,
MK366, NH300
(*Spitfire IX*)
TD341 (*Spitfire XVI*)

2I-W
MK605, ML153 (*Spitfire IX*)
SM512, TB746 (*Spitfire XVI*)

2I-X
MJ799 (*Spitfire IX*)
TB352 (*Spitfire XVI*)
RM689 (*Spitfire XIV*)

2I-Y

2I-Z
NH208 (*Spitfire IX*)

APPENDIX VIII
List of known pilots posted or attached to the Squadron

RAF
C.G. Stevenson, RAF No.1560860, *CANADA*
(later transferred to the RCAF - see RCAF list)

RCAF
J.A. Arsenault, Can./R.174998
W.A. Aziz, Can./J.26930
J.R. Baker, Can./J.42955
R.H. Barbour, Can./R.208178
A.M. Bayly, Can./J.12310
W.J. Bentley, Can./J.18928
P.G. Blades, Can./J.6371
P.G. Bockman, Can./J.40106, *USA*
C.D. Bricker, Can./C.1449
T.S. Burleigh, Can./J.16452
L.J. Burnett, Can./J.21588
J.K. Burns, Can./J.43662
H.C. Charlesworth, Can./J.15146
A.B. Clenard, Can./J.86744
R.J.S. Clow, Can./J.42132
E.J. Collins, Can./R.125040
J. Collins, Can./J.44059

W.G. Conway, Can./J.43780, *USA*
J.H. Cook, Can./J.9454
K.M. Cooke, Can./J.89181
J.C. Copeland, Can./J.9421
W.B. Dalton, Can./J.37005
T.J. De Courcy, Can./J.17641
A.J. Dilworth, Can./J.24247
O.A. Dodson, Can./J.36996
E.H. Fairfield, Can./J.20013
P.E.H. Ferguson, Can./J.40181
H.R. Finlay, Can./J.14030
L.B. Foster, Can./J.27378
H.P. Fuller, Can./J.17752
T.C. Gamey, Can./J.28753
R.L. Gaudet, Can./ R.88145
B.V. Genge, Can./J.23887
W.A.C. Gilbert, Can./J.29310
W.T.H. Gill, Can./J.7766
OA. Godson, Can./J.30996
P.C. Gomm, Can./J.92717, *USA*
W.I. Gould, Can./J.11554
G.J. Grant, Can./R.151192

H.A. Greene, Can./J.44179
R.S. Gurd, Can./R.219163
J.D. Hall, Can./C.1624
H.T. Hallihan, Can./J.8904
H.R. Hanscom, Can J.88672
F.E.W. Hanton, Can./J.10116
R.B. Henderson, Can /J.16753
W.D. Hill, Can./J.35989
R.A. Hodgins, Can./J.41894
A.J. Horrell, Can./J.21413
L.H. Hunt, Can./J.15831
A. Hunter, Can./J.10697
J.R. Irwin, Can./J.11968
G.N. Jermyn, Can./R.181116
F.R. Kearns, Can./J.36358
J. Leyland, Can./J.26993
G.K. Lindsay, Can./J.93439
E.E. Lowry, Can./J.43980
I.R. MacLennan, Can./J.15928
R.D. Marsh, Can./J.16643
W.A.S. Marshall, Can./J.44843
P.C. Martin, Can./J.20646

G.A. **McDonald**, Can./J.42948
J.L. **McMahon**, Can./J.20007
C. **McLean**, Can./C.43775
D.M. **McLeod**, Can./J.4912
S.E. **Messum**, Can./J.19947
K.S. **Meyer**, Can./J.25911
D.A. **Mitchell**, can./J.29891
L.D. **Morrow**, Can./J.36492
T.G. **Munro**, Can./J.24592
G.B. **Murray**, can./J.15476
H.T. **Murray**, Can./21230
J.V. **O'Connor**, Can./J.7014
G.F. **Ockenden**, Can/J.21398
J.D. **Ord**, Can./R.167123
J.W. **O'Tolle**, Can./J.89819
H.F. **Packard**, Can./J.17401
L. **Perez-Gomez**, Can./J.29172, *MEXICO*
R.W. **Perkin**, Can./J.38572
J.M. **Perkins**, Can./J.12880
L.P.E. **Piché**, Can./C.25294
J.C. **Pickering**, Can./R.144095

W.A. **Prest**, Can./J.15101
L.A. **Pyke**, Can./J.42953
V.H. **Rassenti**, Can./J.22462
A. van **Rensselaer-Sainsbury**,
Can./J.25360
M.W. **Richeman**, Can./R.198461
J.S.L. **Robillard**, Can./J.15296
H. **Russel**, Can./J.5818
A.H. **Sager**, Can/J.8638
C.E. **Scarlett**, Can./J.9397
W.V. **Schenk**, Can./J.15072, *USA*
W.J. **Sherman**, Can./J.18283
L.D. **Sherwood**, Can./J.15715
M. **Silver**, Can./J.87984
R.G. **Sim**, Can./J.6947
G.R. **Stephen**, Can./J.18775
C.G. **Stevenson**, Can./C.89550
C. **Stojan**, Can./J.94018
E.B. **Stovel**, Can./J.7815
J.M. **Straile**, Can./J.40982
J.H. **Syrett**, Can./J.38934

G.S. **Taylor**, Can./J.29158
J.H. **Tetros**, Can./J.85709
A.M. **Thomas**, Can./J.42790
J.R. **Thomson**, Can./J.90428
G.W. **Troke**, Can./J.15777
M.C. **Tucker**, Can./J.25144
J.C. **Turcott**, Can./J.18713
H.F. **Ulmer**, Can./J.28739
C.E. **Urquardt**, Can./R.125161
D.M. **Walz**, Can./C.12586
G.B. **Warman**, Can./J.18340
K.B. **Watchorn**, Can./R.195315
T.R. **Watt**, Can./J.10399
D.W.J. **Wegg**, Can./J.39826
J. **Williams**, Can./R.128772
W.I. **Williams**, Can./J.35975
F.A.W.J. **Wilson**, Can./J.85676

APPENDIX IX
ROLL OF HONOUR
✝

AIRCREW

Name	Service No	Rank	Age	Origin	Date	Serial
BENTLEY, William John	Can./J.18928	F/O	24	RCAF	12.08.44	ML303
DE COURCY, Thomas Joseph*	Can./J.17641	S/L	24	RCAF	07.06.45	-
DILWORTH, Arthur Joseph	Can./J.24427	F/O	22	RCAF	25.04.45	TA739
GAMEY, Thomas Clinton	Can./J.28753	F/O	21	RCAF	05.01.45	NH157
HALL, James Dickie	Can./C.1624	S/L	*n/k*	RCAF	16.06.44	MK397
HANSCOM, Harry Robert	Can./J.88672	F/O	22	RCAF	21.04.45	SM664
HORRELL, Arthur James	Can./J.21413	F/O	24	RCAF	11.10.44	NJ669
McLEOD, Henry Wallace	Can./J.4912	S/L	28	RCAF	27.09.44	NH245
MESSUM, Stanley Ernest	Can./J.19447	F/O	29	RCAF	06.04.45	SM670
PICHÉ, Louis Paul Emile	Can./C.25294	F/O	33	RCAF	11.10.44	NJ669
PEREZ-GOMEZ, Luis	Can./J.29172	F/O	21	(MEX)/RCAF	16.06.44	MK607
RUSSEL, Hugh	Can./J.5818	F/L	22	RCAF	16.06.44	NH300

* Killed in a car accident.

Total: 13

Canada: 11, Mexico: 1

GROUNDCREW
None

n/k: not known

Spitfires of No.144 (RCAF) Wing were among the first Spitfires to land on French soil. Clearly identified, MH370 was usually flown by 'Ed' Ferguson during the first stages of Operation 'Overlord'. However the two other Spitfires clearly visible do not wear any codes suggesting that this photo wasn't taken where No.443 Sqn was located at that time. Knowing that MH370 was sent for repairs after being hit by flak on 29.06.44, MH370 might have been seen while in transit after some non-permanent repairs to make it flyable. (*via Chris Thomas*)

Below, taxiing Spitfire Mk.IX MH300/2I-V in June at B.3/St-Croix for another mission (the double '0' of the serial can be seen), a landing strip the Squadron arrived at on the 15th. It was the regular mount of Gordon Ockenden in June 1944 and this photo may have been taken either in the morning of the 16th if Ockenden is sitting in this aircraft, as he flew MH300 on the first mission of the day, or later in the afternoon with F/L Russell in command who didn't come back from this mission, being killed by German fighters which also shot down three other Spitfires of the Squadron. When we watch the French farmers still working like nothing had happened, it is difficult to imagine the war is raging not very far away. (*Author's collection*)

Above:
Some scenes of No.443 Squadron at B.90/Petit Brogel in Belgium at the end of March 1945. At that time, the Squadron was part of No.127 Wing which had also under its control Nos.403, 416 and 421 Canadian Squadrons. The aircraft on dispersal are SM329/2I-T normally flown by P.G. Brockman (USA) and SM512/2I-W 'Klondicke' usually flown by F/O M.J. Clow.
Below:
S/L 'Art' Sager is leading F/O F/L 'Chuck' Charlesworth, Sager in TB476/2I-D 'Ladykiller' and Charlesworth in TB332/2I-N. The latter had been christened as well but the name can't be clearly identified. Sager was in the last days of his command and was about to relinquish command to Thomas De Courcy.
(*both via Chris Thomas*).

A RCAF officer is briefing some Squadron personnel during summer 1945. Behind, Spitfire LF.XVIE TD239/2I-C can be seen (see colour profile), with which S/L De Courcy ashared victory on 03.05.45. It is one of the few XVIEs the squadron had in charge that year. Note the Sky fuselage band has been overpainted.

(via Chris Thomas)

Another view on the ground of Art Sager's aircraft, 2I-D, and 'Chuch' Charlesworth's machine, 2I-N.
(*Author's collection and Chris Thomas*)
Below, '2I-S' taxies in with empty bombs racks and like many Squadrons's aircraft it has been named - in this case 'Ginger'.
(*via Chris Thomas*)

Line-up of the Squadron's Spitfire LF.16s in Germany at the end of summer 1945. Above, TB746/2I-W with a stylised individual letter 'W and the spinner in black/yellow and below 2I-X is believed to be TB352. The latter seems to have a plain spinner. (*via Chris Thomas*)

The last flying equipment of the Squadron was the Spitfire FR.14, but intended to be used as a fighter only. Hence, no camera were taken during flights and the mechanics had no scruples to paint the camera window when they applied the squadron codes (above), even if sometimes they did care (see below). Most of the Spitfire FR.14s were transferred from No.451 (RAAF) Sqn, thus we can still find some unofficial No.451 Sqn badges painted under the cockpit. Note the spirals of the spinner which seems to have been black/yellow - as a hornet - even if on some aircraft it could possibly be white, such as TZ198. (*Brack via Malcolm Laird*)

Even if No.443 Sqn had a short existence, it did have a couple of personalities in its ranks. Above right, 'Art' Sager, a British Columbian, first served with Nos.421 and No.416 Canadian Squadrons during a first tour before starting a second tour with the latter in mid-1944 and eventually joined the unit at the end of September 1944. At that time, his tally had reached six confirmed victories including two shared. However he didn't have the chance to add any more whilst flying with 443 but was awarded a DFC. He completed his second tour in March 1945 and was repatriated to Canada later that summer. Above right Laurent 'Larry' Robillard from Ottawa arrived in mid-1944 after having served with Nos.145 and 72 Sqns during which he claimed four enemy aircraft destroyed, but was shot down once but evaded capture for which he was awarded the DFM. He was posted to Nos.402, 411 and 442 Canadian squadrons during a second tour before joining 443, with which he added three more victories. After the war he served a couple of years with the RCN. Below left, Ian MacLennan from Alberta served first with No.401 (RCAF) Sqn before being posted to Malta to join No.1435 Sqn with which he met considerable successes, claiming seven confirmed victories and was awarded a DFM. Commissioned, he later joined the Squadron for a second tour. However, he was shot down and made a PoW on 07.06.44 before he could add to his tally. Below right, Hartland Finley was a late arrival at the Squadron. He had served previously with Nos.1, 416 (RCAF) and 403 (RCAF) Sqns claiming three confirmed victories, but was lucky enough to add a shared victory in the last days of the war but was himself shot down, but survived. (Authors' collection)

Among the pilots who fought with the Squadron, Luis Perez-Gomez is unique in being one of the very few Mexicans to have served with the RCAF during the war, but the only one to have been killed in action (on 16.06.44). During the same mission, the Squadron lost another pilot, Hugh Russel from Montreal. He had completed a tour with No.416 (RCAF) Sqn in Europe with which he had claimed a confirmed victory off Dieppe during Operation 'Dynamo' in August 1942 before joining 443 for another tour. He was one of the first pilots of the Squadron to shoot down an enemy aircraft, followed by a shared confirmed victory six weeks later.

Gordon Ockenden from Alberta did all his military career with the Squadron, first when it was still named No.127 Sqn, RCAF, following it to Europe. Within a year, he was able to claim five confirmed victories, one being shared, and was awarded a DFC. He remained with the RCAF/CAF after the war reaching the rank of Lieutenant General before retiring. Below right, one of the few Americans to have served with the Squadron, Warren Schenck. Hailing from Pennsylvania, this pilot is also unique as he was a former 'Eagle' pilot and had flown with No.121 (Eagle) Sqn between July and December 1941 but choose to stay in the RCAF and did not transfer to the USAAF. After some second line assignments, he returned as a Flight Lieutenant in Europe and joined the Squadron in February 1944, leaving it at the end of July.

(Authors' collection)

"Wally' McLeod was born in Regina (Sasckatchetwan) and joined the RCAF in September 1940. After his training he was posted overseas and first served with No.132 Sqn in July 1941 and with Nos.485 (NZ) and 602 Sqns by the end of that year. Before 1941 came to an end, he was posted to No.411 (RCAF) Sqn and in May 1942 he sailed for Malta where fame was awaiting him. In Malta he served with No.603 Sqn, then with No.1435 Sqn and in a couple of weeks he became one of the island's top-scorers. In October 1942, he left Malta for England with a DFC ribbon on his chest, soon to be with a Bar. He returned to Canada in 1943 and served as flying instructor at Bagotville (Quebec). In January 1944 he sailed again to the UK to start another tour, taking command of 443 Sqn in March 1944. In the next weeks, he became the unit's top-scorer, shooting down eight enemy aircraft and a well-deserved DSO followed on 05.09.44, by which time he had become the RCAF's top-scorer of the war. Sadly a few days later on 27.09.44, while operating over the Nijmegen area, he failed to return from an engagement with nine Bf109s. At the time of his death, he had claimed 21 aircraft destroyed, three probables and 13 aircraft damaged - one being shared. (*via Hugh Halliday*)

SUMMARY OF THE OPERATIONAL ACTIVITY
No.443 (R.C.A.F.) SQUADRON

A/C types	First sortie	Last sortie	Total sorties	Tot Sub-type	Lost Ops	Lost Acc	A/C lost	Claims	V-1	Pilot †	PoWs	Evad.
SPITFIRE V	-	-	-	-	-	-	-	-	-	-	-	-
SPITFIRE IX	13.04.44	28.03.45	3,781	3,781	20	-	20	36.0	-	6	2	3
SPITFIRE XVI	05.01.45	08.05.45	1,951	1,951	12	5	17	2.0	-	3	1	-
SPITFIRE XIV	-	-	-	-	-	-	-	-	-	-	-	-
Others												
AUSTER V	-	-	-	-	1	-	1	-	-	2	-	-
OTHER CAUSES	-	-	-	-	-	-	-	-	-	1	-	-
COMPILATION	13.04.44	08.05.45	5,732		33	5	38	38.0	-	12	3	3

MAIN AWARDS

DSO: 1

DFC: 5

DFM: -

Points of interest :
- One of the six Canadian Home squadrons to have been sent overseas in 1944.

Unsolved mystery
Flight Commanders list uncompleted.

Statistics :
- Lost one aircraft every 179 sorties - 189 Spitfire IX & 162 for Spitfire XVI.
- Only 8.50 % of the combat aircraft losses until VE-Day occurred during non operational flights.

BADGE
A hornet affronte.

This unit was known as the Hornet Squadron hence the badge.

MOTTO
OUR STING IS DEATH

Authority: King George VI, February 1946

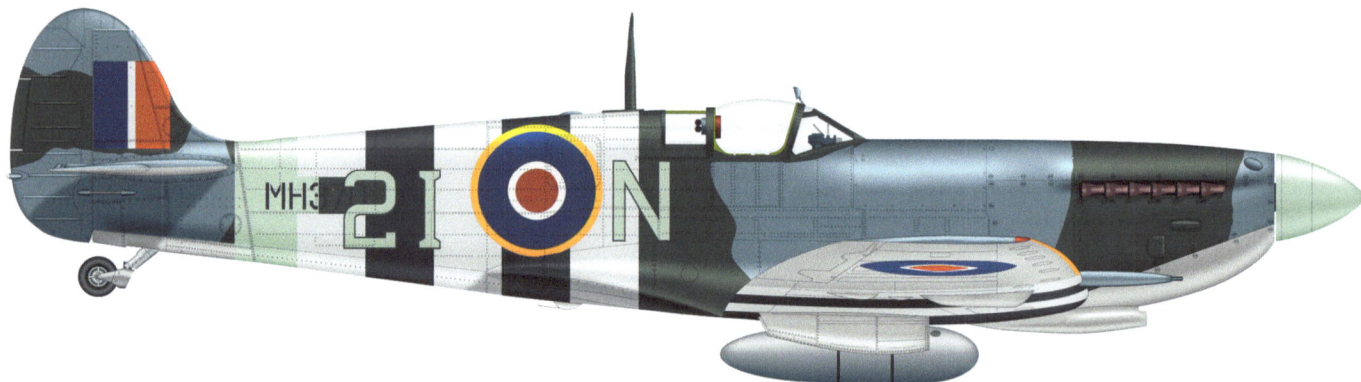

Supermarine Spitfire LF.IX MH370, Flying Officer Percival E.H. 'Ed' Ferguson, B.3/St-Croix (France), June 1944.
MH370 first served with No.485 (NZ) Sqn between August 1943 and March 1944 before being issued the same month to the Squadron as one of the first Spitfires allocated on the 13ᵗʰ. During the first weeks it was flown by various pilots before becoming the mount of F/O 'Ed' Ferguson from May 1944 onwards. On 29.06.44 flown by F/L Alex Hunter during an armed recce in the afternoon, the aircraft's aileron was damaged by flak and the aircraft was sent No.3501 SU for repairs. In September we find it in the inventory of No.322 (Dutch) Sqn but its subsequent fate remains obscure. MH370 has received the standard D-Day markings for June 1944 but the mechanics tried not to overpaint the serial.

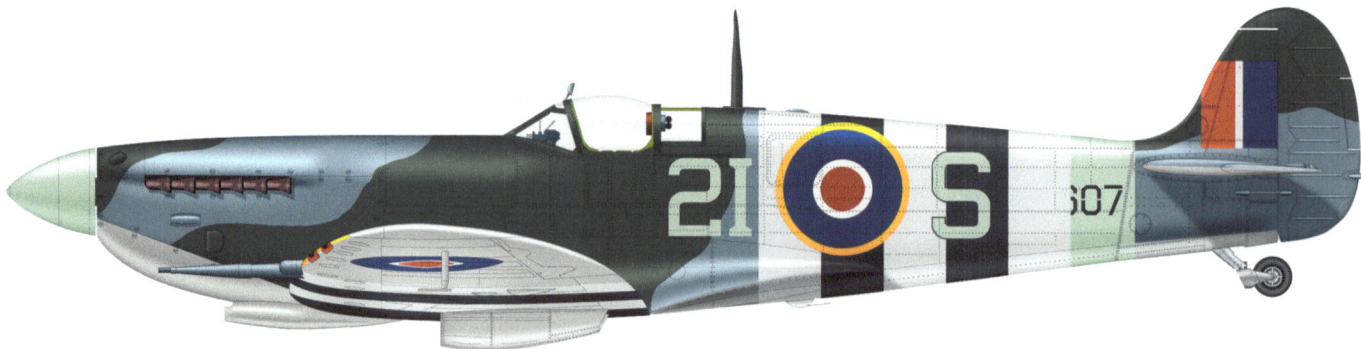

Supermarine Spitfire LF.IX MK607, Flying Officer Luis Perez-Gomez (Mexico), B.3/St-Croix (France), June 1944.
Taken on charge on 29.01.44 at No.9 MU, it was issued to No.443 Sqn on 14.03.44. By June 1944, it had become the mount of F/O Perez-Gomez and he was flying this aircraft when he was shot down and killed on the fateful day 16 June when the Squadon lost four Spitfires against Fw 190s of I./JG 1. Luis Perez-Gomez was one of the few Mexicans to have served in the RCAF during the war, and the only one killed in action in Europe. MK607 has received the standard D-Day markings for June 1944 and it is believed it had the serial over-painted, as with many aircraft of the Squadron.

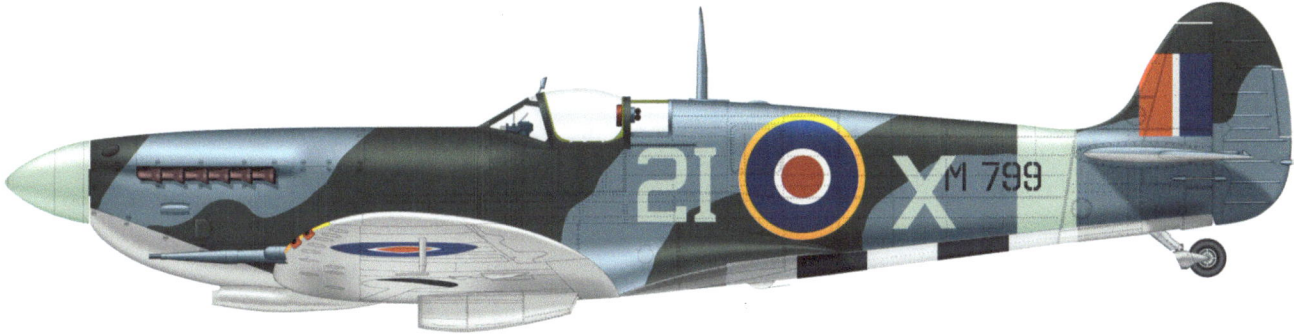

Supermarine Spitfire LF.IX MJ799, Flying Officer Les B. Foster, B.68/Le Culot (France), September 1944.
MJ799 was taken on charge on 28.12.44. It served with Nos.312 (Czech), 453 (RAAF) and 421 (RCAF) Sqns before being taken on Squadron charge in August 1944. During its short stay with the Squadron, it was mainly flown by F/O Forster in September but the Squadron ace Gordon Ockenden claimed two Bf109s on 23.08.44 flying MJ799. In October, it was sent to No.416 (RCAF) Sqn and was eventually sold to Turkey in January 1947. Note the serial partially erased and the D-Day markings now appearing only under the fuselage.

Supermarine Spitfire LF.XVI SM329, Flying Officer Philip G. Bockman (USA), B.90/Petit Brogel (Belgium), March 1945.
SM329 was issued to No.443 Sqn on 18.01.45. It had been taken on charge by the RAF the previous November. In March 1945, SM329 was mainly flown by F/O Bockman, one of few the American pilots who enlisted in the RCAF but who didn't transferred to the USAAF. The markings of the 2nd TAF were sober following the regulations of 03.01.45 with National Markings III (with the outlined yellow circles) - Mk.I converted to Mk.III for the upperwings - in all positions.

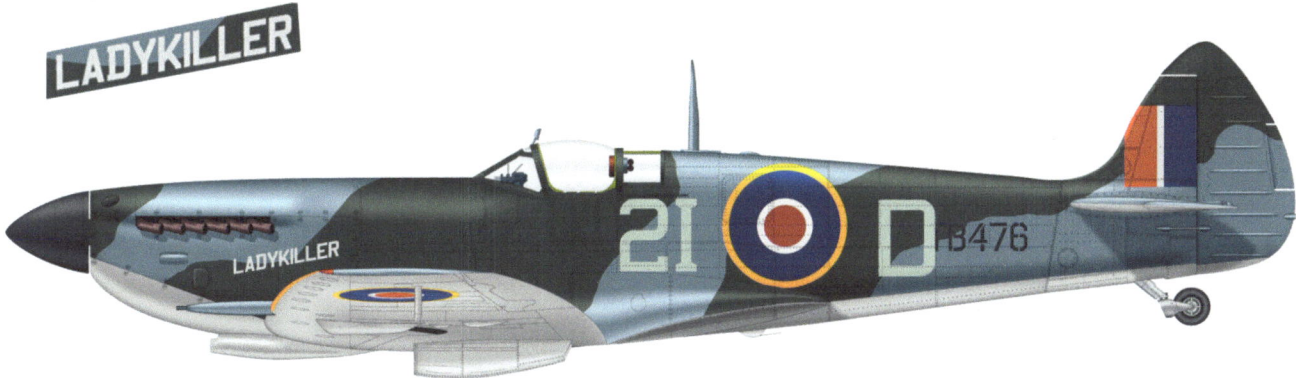

Supermarine Spitfire LF.XVI TB476, S/L Arthur H. 'Art' Sager, B.90/Petit Brogel (Belgium), March 1945.
TB476 was taken on charge on 14.02.45 and issued to the Squadron one month later. From the beginning, it became the mount of the CO, S/L Art Sager, until he left the unit at the end of the month. The aircraft was christened 'Ladykiller'. Later on, it was flown by various pilots and served with the unit until the squadron re-equipped with Spitfire Mk.14s. It seems that it was rather common in the Squadron to give Christian names to the aircraft in Spring 1945.

The two kinds of upper wing roundels painted on 2nd TAF Spitfire Mk.XVIs in 1945, a Mk.I converted to a Mk.III (left) and a Mk.III (right). For the Mk.III, the previous Mk.I had to be overpainted leaving a darker circle around the Mk.III roundel.

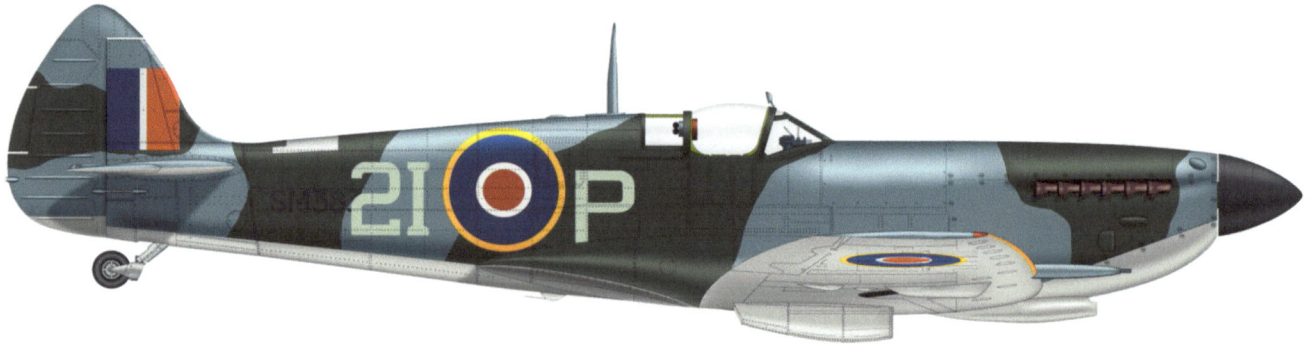

Supermarine Spitfire LF.XVI SM383, Flight Lieutenant Robert D. March, B.100/Goch (Germany), April 1945.
SM383 was taken on charge at No.6 MU on 09.11.44. In January it was issued to No.416 (RCAF) Sqn and one month later to No.443 Squadron. In the next few months it was regularly flown by F/L March. On 21.04.45 March was flying SM383 on an armed recce during which the aircraft was hit by flak, obliging the pilot to bale out. Note that SM383 seems to have been hit a previous time as a part of the fuselage near the tail had been already replaced and left unpainted.

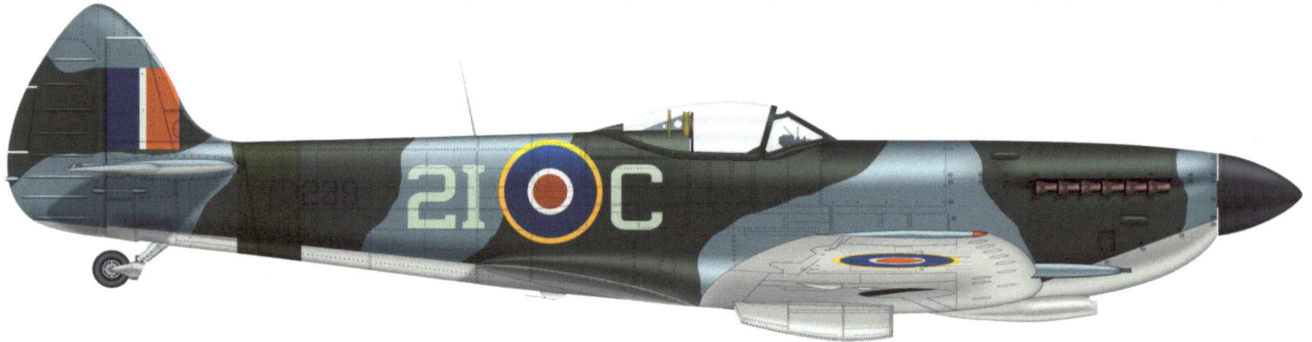

Supermarine Spitfire LF.XVIE TD239, S/L Thomas J. De Courcy, B.154/Reinsehlen (Germany), June 1945.
TD239 is one of the few Spitfire LF.XVIEs with a bubble canopy to have flown with the Squadron. TD239 was taken on charge on 27.03.45 at No.9 MU and issued to the Squadron somewhere early in May 1945 even if on the movement card the date is 05.07.45. While flying this aircraft S/L De Courcy claimed a shared victory on 03.05.45. TD239 served with the 443 until the Squadron was re-equipped with FR.XIVs. Note the fuselage band was clearly over-painted. This aircraft found its way to Greece later on. (see photo p.18)

Supermarine Spitfire LF.XVI TB746, B.174/Utersen (Germany), Autumn 1945.
TB746 served briefly with No.66 Sqn during the last two weeks of the war and when the unit was recalled to the UK, the aircraft was eventually issued to No.443 Sqn on 21.06.45. Note the style of the individual letter 'W' and the spinner, distinctive markings used by the squadron in the late stages of its existence to represent the colour of an hornet, black/yellow. (see photo p.20)

Supermarine Spitfire LF.XVIE TD341, B.174/Utersen (Germany), Autumn 1945.
A late production Spitfire LF.XVIE, TD341 was taken on RAF charge on 12.04.45. It was issued to the Squadron on 03.05.45 but arrived too late to participate in the last missions. It is seen later at the end of summer or early in autumn with the spinner painted in black and yellow and the unofficial badge showing an hornet. After the Squadron was re-equipped with Spitfire XIVs, TD341 was stored and eventually scrapped in July 1946.

Supermarine Spitfire FR.XIV NH922, B.174/Utersen (Germany), January 1946.

No.443 Sqn inherited aircraft from No.451 (RAAF) Sqn, including NH922 which was taken on charge on 03.05.45 and issued to the Australian squadron in October 1945. If the squadron code letters have been changed, the identity of the former user, No.451 Sqn can be seen with the unofficial badge painted under the cockpit. Note also the spinner representing a hornet, black/yellow. NH922 became SG-101 with the Belgian Air Force when it was sold to that country.

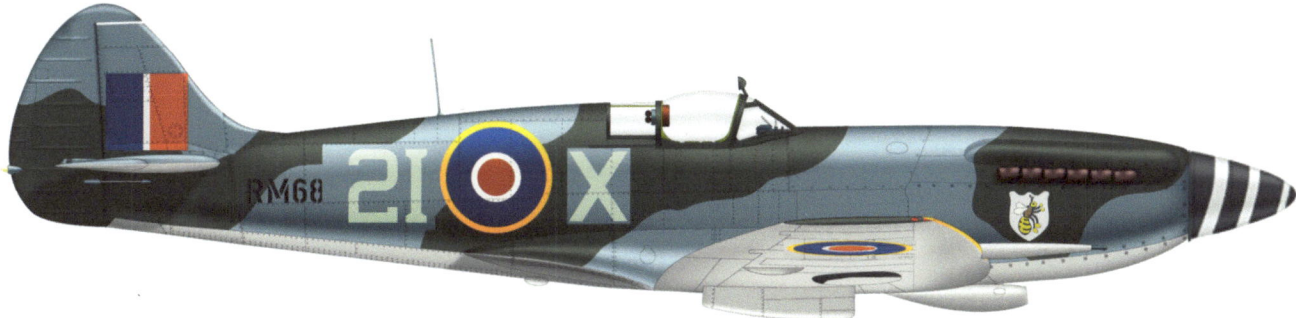

Supermarine Spitfire F.XIV RM689, B.174/Utersen (Germany), January 1946.

Taken on charge on 03.07.44 at No.39 MU, it was used for various trials before being issued to an operational unit, No.350 (Belgian) Sqn, in March 1945. In January 1946, RM689 was sent to the Squadron for re-equipment and the Squadron's codes were painted on over the former ones, explaining the re-touched paint squares around the letters. The unofficial Squadron badge was also applied on the nose. In March 1945 within the 2nd TAF, RM689 should have Mk.III National markings under the wings, but they might have been replaced later on by the standard underwing roundels without the yellow circle. The spinner appears to be black and white suggesting that the aircraft had arrived recently at the squadron and the spirals were inherited from the former owner. The white is believed to have been changed for yellow soon afterwards. RM689 survived after the war, becoming a warbird later on.

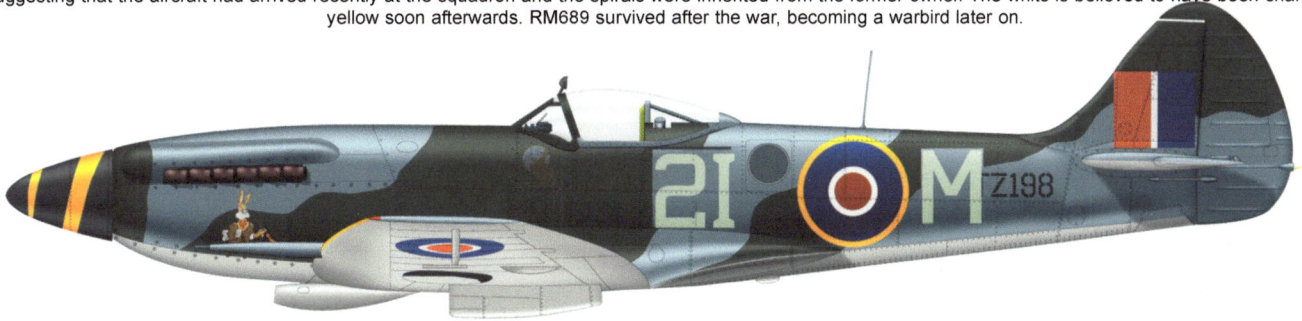

Supermarine Spitfire FR.XIV TZ198, B.174/Utersen (Germany), January 1946.

One of the last Spitfire Mk.XIVs to have been built, it was taken on RAF charge on 18.06.45, stored before being issued to No.451 (RAAF) Sqn early in September and consequently to No.443 in January 1946. Here too, the former unit's codes were over-painted as well the unofficial Australian emblem painted under the cockpit which is seen faded out. Note the personal artwork, a bunny which was coming from an Australian pilot. It is not know if the latter was kept by the Canadian pilots over the next two months

Close-ups of the Bugs Bunny (left) of TZ198, the unofficial Hornet of the Squadron (above) and the 451 Squadron's unofficial badge on the right.

SQUADRON

USN AIRCRAFT 1922-

The Supermarine
SPITFIRE Mk.V
in the Far East

Vo
Type Desig

Phil H. LISTEMANN

Fighter Leaders
of the RAF, RAAF, RCAF, RNZAF & SAAF in WW2

Volume I

Phil H. Listemann

RAF, DOMINION & ALLIED SQUADRONS
AT WAR:
STUDY, HISTORY AND STATISTICS

No.137 Squadron
1941 - 1945

PHIL H. LISTEMANN

SQUADRONS!
No.2

The Republic
Thunderbolt Mk.I

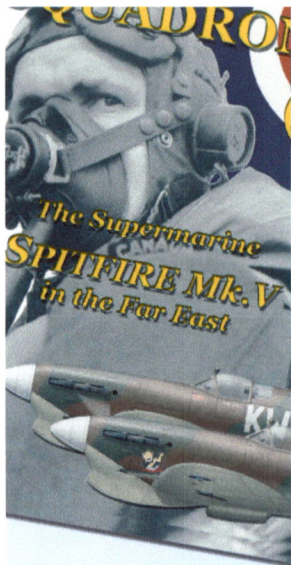

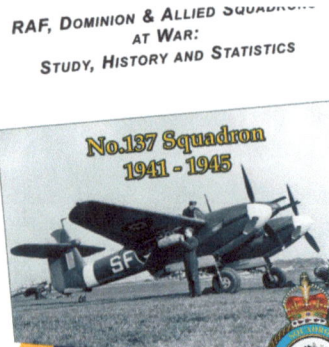

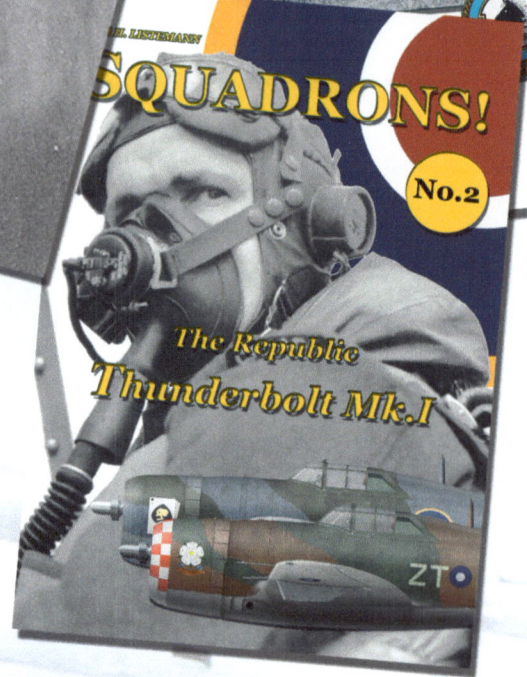

www.RAF-IN-COMBAT.com

- USN Aircraft 1922-1962 -
- Squadrons! -
- RAF, Dominion and Allied squadrons at War -
- Allied Wings -
- Famous squadrons of WW2 -
- Fighter Leaders -

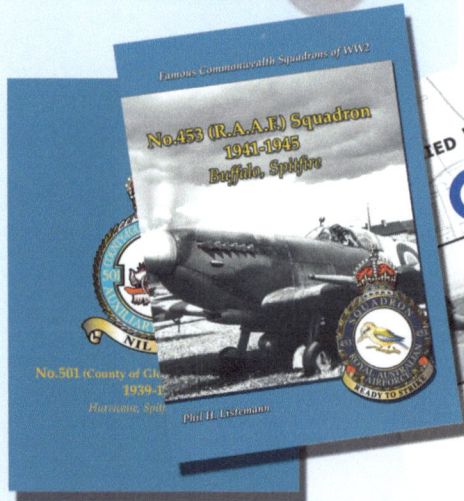

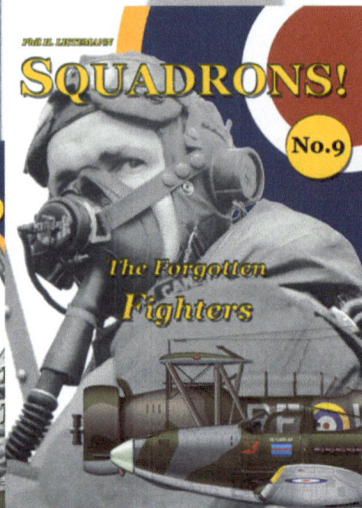

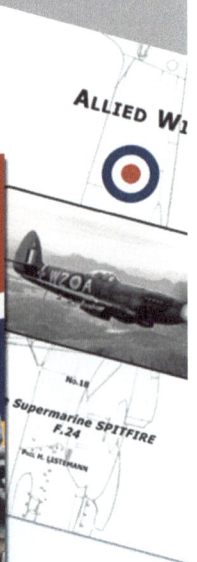

RAF, DOMINION & ALLIED SQUADRONS
AT WAR:
STUDY, HISTORY AND STATISTICS

ALLIED W

Famous Commonwealth Squadrons of WW2

No.453 (R.A.A.F.) Squadron
1941-1945
Buffalo, Spitfire

No.501 (County of Gl
1939-1
Hurricane, Sp

Phil H. Listemann

No.151 (County of Kent) Squadron
1941 - 1945

LIED WINGS

Phil H. LISTEMANN

SQUADRO

Phil H. LISTEMANN

SQUADRONS!
No.9

The Forgotten
Fighters

No.18
Supermarine SPITFIRE
F.24
Phil H. LISTEMANN

Short SIN

The Handley
Halifax